APPETITE

PITT POETRY SERIES

Ed Ochester, Editor

APPETITE • AARON SMITH

For Reggie –

So nice to finally put a face with a name!

Aaron

3/19/14

NYC

UNIVERSITY OF PITTSBURGH PRESS

Published by the University of Pittsburgh Press, Pittsburgh, Pa., 15260

Copyright © 2012, Aaron Smith

Manufactured in the United States of America

Printed on acid-free paper

10 9 8 7 6 5 4 3 2 1

ISBN 13: 978-0-8229-6219-9

ISBN 10: 0-8229-6219-5

for Brandon Belcher, who knows all of this and more

CONTENTS

5. APPETITE

I • MEN IN GROUPS

Histories of men I haven't met
are waving good-bye from cabs.

—REGINALD SHEPHERD

Men in Groups

take their shirts off and chase basketballs across city pavement. They say
nice block and *good job, man* and *dude*. They're electric. They're sweating.
Men in groups find someone to pick on, someone they like or don't like—

it doesn't matter—fat or slow or stupid or smart. *Hey retard! Hey faggot!*
They talk about *tits*—who's touched them and hasn't—or they don't talk
or listen or smile. They touch hands in huddles and pray into helmets,

smack asses, *good game*. Men in groups carry caskets. Men in groups stare
at women. They wear backward hats and backward glances. Throw rocks
and punches, drop bricks off bridges. They flex. *Same as me* is their motto.

Men in groups spray-paint walls, smash windows. Men in groups hurt
women in woods. Men in groups take their shirts off and dance. Men
in groups carry guns. Are brave. Are cowards. Are solemn and crazy

and lonely. Men in groups hurt men in woods. Men in groups clear
sidewalks. Men in groups are locked up. Men in groups stare at men.
Men in groups pull their pants down. Men in groups slam their fists down.

Safe

We weren't supposed to touch
      the guns lined up
under our parents' bed, rifles
      for hunting, pistols *for protecting*
our home. The carpet was burning
      lava, we'd dangle our feet,
the barrels mysterious beneath us.
      Headstands on the floor,
inches from accident, from sadness,
      and always we knew not to tell.
Nobody home, I lay my body the length
      of the bed, all the barrels
facing out. I pressed my back against
      their silent ends, metal tips
poking neck and spine—a firing squad!
      a stickup! Sometimes I'd face
them, a microphone, or love
      their tiny lips—tongue-deep
between my teeth—practicing the kiss
      the way my sister used her fist.

Lucky

Apparently there was a line you crossed
        thin as Kenny's stream of piss
when he stood too far from the urinal
        and poor Jeremy Simms walked through it.
Who knew they'd punish you for knowing
        your turquoise shirt went perfectly

with black sweatpants and turquoise
        Chuck Taylors? Everyone laughed
and laughed because Kenny pissed on Jeremy,
        and that was, even you had to admit,
funny. And someone must have thought
        it was funny when the new kid Dean

thought you were a girl in the bathroom. You'd
        spoken too loudly or acted too happy
with your turquoise outfit and hair-sprayed hair.
        He thought you were a girl and told everyone.
Because they had hair under their arms,
        they turned on you. But you were lucky

they never made you lick the toilet like that one kid
        or stand in the middle of the room
with your pants down. They never made you say
        faggotcocksucker was your name.
You were lucky you were only laughed at.
        Lucky they never did that.

Fatal Attraction, 1987 (Movie Review and Trivia)

It was before caller ID
when you could still hassle the married man
who knocked you up
and wouldn't leave his wife
and her textbook hair.

The world was gauzy,
city-smudged,
seen through a powdery sheen.
Buttery sunshine behind the movie-magic downpour!

I said, *Look, Steven, it's not really raining.
It's sunny in the background.*

Then Michael Douglas with cream cheese on his lips.
Then pants around his ankles.
Then he and Glenn Close fucking on the sink
(water pouring out beneath her ass).

A blow job in an elevator
(we only see their feet).

If you ever come near my family again, I'll kill you!

I won't be ignored!

Crazy smiles
more phone calls and build and build and
deadrabbitdeadrabbitdeadrabbit

• Glenn Close (Alex) took
the script to two psychiatrists
to ask if her character's behavior
was possible.

• Barbara Hershey, Miranda
Richardson, and Debra Winger
all turned down the role of Alex.

• *Fatal Attraction* received six
Academy Award nominations,
including Best Picture,
but won no awards.

Fat Ass

The woman in the next cubicle: fat ass,
the man on the train: fat ass, the director
of the nonprofit where I work
(though always dieting): fat ass
and a bitch. Me on my fourth cookie:
fat ass. My mom in her chair: fat ass.
My dad in his chair (reclining): fat ass,
and my sister (though she'll never forgive me).
Jeremy, Annie, Brian, Lois, Chip, Jan,
Nancy, David Groff and David Trinidad:
all fat asses. My editor: fat ass. The employees
of my publishing company (if I still have one)—
every single one of them—a fat ass.
Louise Glück, Ted Kooser, Charles Simic:
fat ass, fat ass, fat ass. Robert Pinsky,
Rita Dove, Billy Collins: fat ass, fat ass, really
really fat ass. David Lehman: Best American
Fat Ass. Jesus fat ass. The devil fat ass.
The fat ass pope in his extra big fat ass robe.

Psalm (Queer)

Mom held the belt
in her hand, said she could

smack my face over
and over and enjoy it.

Yes, she really said that.
Yes, she loved God that much.

Hurtful

It's true I've never been able to defend
myself against your white T-shirt
and that for most of last summer

I confused wanting you
with wanting not to be lonely.

There are four words

in the English language that have
no rhymes: *orange, month, silver,*

and *purple*. I want more than anything
to prove that wrong, and the closest
I've come is *hurtful*.

So let me clarify: Finally,
I do not love you. Who
could take a lifetime

of your bad poetry? However,

there are things I hate you
more for: That you can eat french fries

and not exercise. That everyone you let
be close to you has to need
you. Strangers gawking

because you're radiant
(and you are radiant!)

Jesus Poem (Pierre et Gilles)

He's whimsical in feathers
(Always in glitter!)

A very sad very pout-
Y Ganymede on a rock with a rock

Body and big rock
Down his G-string.

He's a fifties housewife
With a coaster stain of lipstick,

A let-me-service-you grin.
He's several shirtless men

Against brick walls.
A sexy shiny saint,

A crying sailor.

Fire Island, June 2008

I wanted Steven to go on, so I said *go on,*
and he did. And I stood on the sand, on a strip
of land, water and night sky in front of me,
water and night sky behind, the stars strung
like bulbs too small to be useful. I was moving away
next month, trying to slow everything down. Behind black sky
there is more black sky. I said, *remember this,*
so I'd remember. *You're still going to die one day,* and I will.

Spring Rush

The college boys have pulled their shirts
    off and are playing football
on the lawn. Their farmer tans pink
    in the afternoon sun. They toss

and jog, slight fake and almost
    tackle. One puts his face too close
to another one's stomach, grabs
    the guy's waist—steady—to keep

from falling; then a damp armpit on the back
    of his neck, as a blond wraps his arm
around him in a quick guy-hug. I am old-
    er and pretend not to see, furtive

in sunglasses, looking at them, past
    them, at them. I could ruin the game
by watching the *wrong* way—professor gawking
    at students; even a shift between them

could change everything: a hand more than
    smacking an ass, someone pressed too long
against a humid chest. Crash of skin,
    body pushing body into perfect crush.

Their biceps bulge, un-bulge, bulge again.
    It's not that I want them. I've had enough
men, and yet I can't stop looking at them
    while trying not to look at them.

I'm blind to the world and he's turning me
over and over.

—DAVID WOJNAROWICZ

Sometimes I Want a Gun

My friend Michael hates the movie *Titanic*:
Do we really need more celebrations of heterosexual love?

My mother hates the movie because of Kate Winslet's breasts.
(She actually calls it the boob movie!)

Did she have to go topless?
I was so embarrassed sitting there with your dad!
Can you imagine if your sister did that?

When my sister's friends were getting pregnant in high school,
my mother said to her:

Not only would I be embarrassed you were pregnant,
but I'd be so upset that you did "it."

(I like *Titanic*. I saw it twice in the theater
and watch it every time it's on TBS.)

• • •

I learned the word *gay* from television.
"Gay cancer" was on the news:

> Men holding hands, then those same men
> on doctor tables: needles in their arms,

> white gloves pressing their stomachs,
> sores on their bodies.

I was afraid the feelings I had
meant I was gay.

I didn't want to, but I had to tell mom.
I had to find out if god could save me,
could keep me from getting sick.

If god makes someone gay,
can he also make them not gay?

(I begged her not to tell dad.)

My mother said: *Rebuke the devil in the name of Jesus.*
It's just the devil putting bad thoughts in your head.

I said: *But it's not just thoughts, it's feelings, too.*
She said: *Rebuke the devil over and over,*
a thousand times if you have to.
God can heal you.
God won't let someone be gay
who doesn't want to be.

(I was eight.)

If you keep having those "thoughts,"
try harder.

• • •

Tony Danza taking his shirt off on *Who's the Boss?*
       (*I rebuke you, satan, in the name of jesus*)

Male strippers on *Geraldo* and *Donahue*
Shirtless *Solid Gold* dancers
       (*I rebuke you, satan, in the name of jesus*)

The men my dad played basketball with
       (*I rebuke you, satan, in the name of jesus*)

Jason Clover
       (*I rebuke you, satan*)

• • •

When I told mom the thoughts wouldn't stop,
she told my dad, called him home
from the plant to talk to me.

I knew he would spank me
like he did when I failed swimming lessons,
when I chose the beating over drowning.

(Years later: *I thought you'd be more afraid of me*
than the water.)

16

My father said two things:

    1) *Don't tell your mom about this again.*

    2) *Does it bother you when I take my shirt off?*

• • •

In college a woman got on top of me topless.
Her breasts on my mouth (my mouth closed).

I wasn't disgusted. I just *was*. Indifferent.
She just was, and there was nothing more.

The next morning I drove to the river,
wrote a suicide note.

• • •

The woman on the train
keeps shoving her ass against my shoulder.
She's standing. I'm sitting down.

Her boyfriend has backed her against the railing.
He keeps opening his mouth and putting it on her face.
I hear their mouth sounds, and I hate them.

I want to say something cliché like: get a room.
I want to say something like: you take for granted
how easy you have it. Sometimes I want a gun.

• • •

It would upset me
for a woman to see my penis.

It would seem like a lot of pressure
to have the only penis in the room.

It's more natural
that same would be with same.

• • •

As a kid in the car with my family,
the radio said there was a gay pride parade in New York City.

Dad said: *Wouldn't it be funny to walk down the street*
with a poster that says: Hooray for AIDS!

(*I rebuke you, satan, in the name of jesus*)

• • •

A woman on the street last week
had the most beautiful breasts.

Her face wasn't pretty. Her outfit wasn't pretty,
but her breasts pushed up and out,

were romance-novel creamy.
I thought: I almost get it.

Steven once said: *I could sleep with a woman if she had a perfect body.*
I thought: that's big of you.

• • •

I was sixteen the first time I made myself orgasm.
I jerked off to a guy in swimming trunks

on the cover of J. Crew catalog.
I stared at the place where the hair

disappeared into his waistline.
I knew I had damned myself to hell,

was turned over to a reprobate mind.
I begged god to take me back.

(*I rebuke you, satan, in the name of jesus*)

I said: *Send me a sign to show you forgive me.*
I would have called the slightest breeze his presence.

Film Short: Husband and Wife in a Grocery Store

Irene says she needs something sweet,
something other than Krispy Kremes
which upset her stomach. (Irene was my teacher
and now we're standing in a grocery store.)
How did we get from late papers and me coming out
to angel food cake vs. chocolate,
to the men we've slept with and her cancer?

>I say: *I can't believe we're here, this feels like a movie.*
>She says: *We could be husband and wife!*
>I say: *Can you imagine how we'd film it?*

>We'd drive my jeep to Kroger.
Irene would rub a plum: *I bet they look better than they taste.*
I'd say: *I can't believe you were my teacher*
and now we're standing in a grocery store!
We'd pick out an angel food cake.

>—Cut to us sitting at her table, she's telling
that story about how all Buddhists are into fisting,
>we're laughing
>—(nobody is sick)—
>grabbing handfuls of cake, eating it.

He Only Reads Fiction

Since green has never looked good on him, you tell him he should wear green. You say, *the palm of the earth is green*, and because he's sentimental (and only reads popular fiction) he loves it. You convince him to buy green towels. (*You can never have too many green towels!*) You push him toward green mugs and plates, utensils with green plastic handles. (You want his whole world to become unflattering.) He says, *green as the trees in the forest*, and he's proud of his simile. You tell him to write that down, publish it. *Yes, love, it really is that good.* Green pants and green shirts and green plants for his windowsill. Green knobs for his doors! Green rugs for his floor! Green socks and green boots to walk around in!

Celebrity Photo (Daniel Craig w/ Angelina Jolie)

quod me nutrit me destruit

The woman he's with
has death tattooed on her stomach,
the woman he's with makes headlines
for cutting her arms, for kissing
her brother, for a vial of blood
around her neck. She's too
lippy, too breasty, too child adopty
for some. And he's looking away.
He wants to say:

The light on your forehead has nothing to do with God

or

If you were dead, you'd green-glow like a morgue

or

What would it be like to kiss your brother

He doesn't want to be in front of the marquee,
ignored by her side. He thinks:

I'll never be a big star, will I ever be a big star?

It's before the no-neck muscles,
the double-stuffed Speedo,
before the paparazzi outside his door.

The necklace he's wearing is cheap
(red, green, purple plastic).
He looks like a country singer.
He could sing those songs
about boots and booty, his honky-tonk baby,
God bless America, don't let
the unborn babies die.

The Problem with Straight People
(What We Say Behind Your Back)

Max after the art opening:

Sometimes I hate straight people so much
I want to kill them. That's why
I don't write. I can't say that in a book
and that's all I want to say.

Brandon on the phone:

We should start straight bashing.
Find an asshole straight guy
and beat him with a bat,
fuck him in the ass.

Gang up on straight couples
kissing on the train.
Tell them to take
their disgusting lifestyle somewhere else.

I know it's not right, but I'm tired
of making everyone comfortable.
Do you know how many times
I've been called faggot in New York?

Celeste yesterday:

Fuck straight women who don't think
what we do is fuck,
and fuck straight women who don't ask
about my lover!

Sara's e-mail:

I just want to hold Michele's hand
without straight men yelling out the car window.
Can one thing in the world
have nothing to do with them?
I'd like to rip their balls off!

Michele's e-mail:

I want to scream at my co-workers:
"Yes, we're lesbians! No, we don't want to have a baby!"

Tim at G Lounge:

I hate straight girls in gay bars,
thinking they can be as rude as they want
because nobody here wants to sleep with them,
like our world's not real to them,
like we're not real!

Steven at lunch:

Straight people will only go so far,
and then they'll turn on you.
There's always some line, some point
where you're on your own.
You'll be too gay, too prissy,
too loud, too something.

Me right now:

I hate straight students who look disgusted once they figure out I'm gay.
I hate straight men who imitate my voice when they think I can't hear them.
I hate straight men who make their wrists limp when they think I can't see them.
I hate straight men who joke about bending over for soap in the shower.
I hate straight men who have sex with men.
I hate straight women who say, "It's such a waste that you're gay."
I hate straight people who say, "I don't understand why you're so angry."

Boogie Nights, 1997 (Movie Review and Trivia)

If you tell your son he's stupid, he'll use
His monster dong for evil
Instead of good.

If you drop out of school,
You'll be forced to skate naked through the world—
They'll call you Rollergirl.

Good drugs, nice Italian shoes, and thirteen inches
Can't make a guy happy.

Sex is bad. Sex is bad
If you film it and like it and are good at it.

Sex is good and porn really *can* change lives.

Women who snort coke and fuck will lose their children.

Black pornographers have a hard time
Getting small business loans.

• Leonardo DiCaprio was offered
the role of Dirk Diggler, but he'd
already agreed to be in *Titanic*.
He suggested Mark Wahlberg.

• The TK421 stereo modification
Buck Swope (Don Cheadle)
mentions is also the call sign for
the stormtrooper Luke Skywalker
impersonates on the Death Star
in *Star Wars*.

• The name Amber Waves (Julianne
Moore's character) was used as
a porn name once before in an
episode of *Night Court*.

After All These Years You Know They Were Wrong about the Sadness of Men Who Love Men

It's Palm Springs and you've slipped away
from a day of swimming and drinking to lie
for a minute with your eyes closed
in the other room while the air-conditioner
moan-groans outside the window—your body
chilled from sunburn and untouched
for months. Startled from near sleep
you hear a crash
of laughter, man-laughter, the slapping
of bare backs, hands smacking
the skin of men drying
by the pool or making hamburgers
in the kitchen or solving a puzzle
on the glass table in twilight—
Does anybody need another drink?
and laughter. *The pizza's here;*
Can I have a cigarette?
Pass the pretzels and your name:
Has anyone seen Aaron?
You don't say anything but listen to the man
saying your name—Soon someone will be sent
to look for you, and you'll pretend
to be sleeping, say you must have dozed off,
you'll rejoin the party soon but need
another minute. You want
to remember this. You've waited
your whole life for them to miss you.

3 · I LOVE THE PART

Today I am truly horribly upset because
Marilyn Monroe died, so I went to a
matinee B-movie and ate King Kong
popcorn.

—JOE BRAINARD

I love the part in *Casino Royale* where Daniel Craig is tied naked to a chair, and the guy who is about to torture him says, "Wow, you've taken good care of your body." It's almost as gay as the part where he emerges from the water in the blue Speedo.

I love the part in *Dead Man Walking* where Susan Sarandon is crying through the bars of Sean Penn's jail cell, but she's also kind of making an orgasm face.

I love the part in *American Beauty* where Chris Cooper is wet and kisses Kevin Spacey in the garage. It's cliché for the military guy to be closeted, but it's still really hot.

I love the part in *Magnolia* where Julianne Moore is crying in the lawyer's office, "I've sucked other men's cocks." I love that when she says the word "cocks" she sounds like she could be retarded. I feel bad for thinking that, but it's true.

I love the part in *Magnolia* where Tom Cruise has his pants at his ankles, and his penis flops to the left in his white briefs. It looks so big I can't stop staring at it. I wonder if it's fake.

I love the part in *My Own Private Idaho* where River Phoenix gets blown by the lumpy man, and the barn falls and shatters in the road. It's hard to enjoy it, though, because I can't stop thinking: he's dead.

I love the part in *Moonstruck* where Cher is kicking the can, but the red sports car parked on the street is distracting.

I love the part in *The History Boys* where Dominic Cooper hits on his teacher. Joe said he jerked off to it twice. (My friend Matt admitted he jerked off to the rape scene in *The Accused*: "I knew she wasn't really being raped, and that one guy had a nice ass.")

I love the part in *Good Will Hunting* where Robin Williams makes Matt Damon cry by repeating "It's not your fault." Sometimes I say that to my friends, but I don't think they get the joke.

I love the part in *Titanic* where Kate Winslet slogs through water to rescue Leonardo DiCaprio. She jumps off the boat, back on the boat. She turns around, and her makeup is perfect.

I love the part in *Titanic* where Gloria Stuart throws the necklace into the ocean, and her toenails are painted bright red!

I love the part in *As Good as It Gets* where Greg Kinnear says his father told him not to come home again because he was gay. I don't know if it's a good scene, or if I just like it because I'm gay.

I love the part in *The Transporter* where Jason Statham just *has* to take his shirt off to fight.

I love the part in *Transporter 3* where Jason Statham just *has* to take his shirt off to fight.

I love the part in *Transporter 3* where the woman makes Jason Statham do a striptease. It's sexy because he's angry and doesn't want to do it.

I love the part in *Crank* where Jason Statham is wearing a hospital gown and stands up with a hard-on on a stolen motorcycle. (I love that they play the *Midnight Cowboy* song.)

I love the part in *Unfaithful* where Diane Lane is giddy on the train after having sex with Olivier Martinez. I used to feel like that after seeing my chiropractor. I was totally in love with him, but he married someone else.

I love the part in *The Wizard of Oz* where they all get makeovers.

I love the part in *Little Children* where Kate Winslet and Patrick Wilson fuck in the basement, and while they're fucking, she slaps his ass. (I love that Patrick Wilson is naked!)

I love the part in *Watchmen* where Patrick Wilson is naked.

I love the part in *Hard Candy* where Patrick Wilson is naked.

I love the part in *Passengers* where Patrick Wilson is naked.

I love the part in *Beaches* where Bette Midler has to leave rehearsal because Barbara Hershey is dying. I love when she yells, "Diana! Diana, get my bag!" It sounds so glamorous.

I love the part in *A Single Man* where Colin Firth tries to figure out the best way to shoot himself in the head. It made me think of my father's father who killed himself and how the police said he shot himself twice because the first time didn't do it.

I love the part in *The Color Purple* where Whoopi Goldberg reunites with her sister and children. It's so emotional, but when her children speak you don't know what they're saying because they can't speak English. So you're crying, but you're also like, huh?

I love the part in *Showgirls* where Elizabeth Berkley runs out of the room.

I love the part in *Showgirls* where Elizabeth Berkley runs out of the room. (There are a lot of those parts.)

I love the part in *The Silence of the Lambs* where Jodie Foster examines the body, and the murder victim's name is Frederica Bimmel. It's sad that she was murdered and sad that she was named that.

I love the part in *The Silence of the Lambs* where Jodie Foster finds the woman in the pit, and the woman screams: "Don't you leave me here you fucking bitch." I understand she's scared, but I don't think it's very smart to call the person who's trying to save you a fucking bitch.

I love the part in *Seven* where Gwyneth Paltrow's head is in a box. I wish she would be murdered in every movie. I have to admit I liked her in *Iron Man*, but mostly when she ran in her strappy, high-heeled shoes.

I love the part in *Far from Heaven* where Dennis Quaid kisses the man. A woman I worked with said the guy he kissed was her cousin, but I think she was lying.

I love the part in *Steel Magnolias* where Sally Field says, "Oh, God, I wanna know why? WHHHYYYYY?" The first time I saw that movie there was a fly on the screen on her boob.

I love the part in *Raging Bull* when Cathy Moriarty walks out of the bathroom, and you can see her gigantic panties under her nightgown. When Robert De Niro tells her to take them off, it takes her a long time to step out of them.

I love the part in *Infamous* where Daniel Craig and the other criminal shoot the family. It's hard to watch, but the guy who plays the son looks good shirtless and tied up.

I love the part in *Alice Doesn't Live Here Anymore* where Jodie Foster, as a little kid, is more butch than Harvey Keitel who's hunky and breaking windows.

I love the part in *Deliverance* where Jon Voight breaks down crying at the table and the old woman keeps talking about her 12 ½ inch cucumber. (I also love that Burt Reynolds wears a sleeveless, zip-up, black rubber vest and says deep things while holding a bow and arrows.)

I love the part in *Making Love* where Michael Ontkean leaves Kate Jackson and lives with his boyfriend in an apartment in New York City. They wear soft colors, have Ken-doll hair, and say words like "kiddo."

I love the part in *Working Girl* where Melanie Griffith catches Alec Baldwin in bed with the character named Doreen. I just saw the movie again on Showtime and wanted Melanie Griffith to call her "Whoreen."

I love the part in *Working Girl* where Melanie Griffith is trying to talk numbers with Harrison Ford, but she can't concentrate because really she just wants him inside her.

I love the part in *Brokeback Mountain* where Jake Gyllenhaal is trying to talk sheep with Heath Ledger, but he can't concentrate because really he just wants him inside him. I don't actually remember a part like that, but I do love the part where Heath Ledger spits on his hand.

I love the part in *Chinatown* where Jack Nicholson and Faye Dunaway are in bed and her face is near his gorilla armpit. I love that when she sits beside him we can see her nipples. I felt like I shouldn't be seeing Faye Dunaway's nipples.

I love the part in *Ordinary People* where we see the choir singing. It reminds me how singing in choir made me feel like a total fag. Not in the gay-fag way, but in the fag-fag way.

32

I love the part in *Waiting to Exhale* where Angela Bassett tells her husband that she can't believe he's leaving her for a white woman. He says, "Would it help if she was black?" She says, "No. It would help if you were black."

I love the part in *Pee-wee's Big Adventure* where Paul Reubens says, "There's a lotta things about me you don't know anything about, Dottie. Things you wouldn't understand. Things you couldn't understand."

I love the part in *Thelma and Louise* where Geena Davis pulls her suitcase to the pool. I never understood why she took her suitcase to the pool.

I love the part in *Boys Don't Cry* where Chloë Sevigny brushes her hair, but it doesn't matter because it's really bad hair.

I love the part in *The Exorcist*: "Keep away. The sow is mine."

I love the part in *Death Becomes Her*: "My ass! I can *see* my *ass!*"

I love the part in *Pulp Fiction*: "Bring out the gimp."

I love the part in *Erin Brockovich*: "Bite my ass, Kripsy Kreme."

I love the part in *Waiting for Guffman*: "I just hate you, and I hate your ass face."

I love the part in *Sixteen Candles*: "I can't believe I gave my panties to a geek."

I love the part in *An Education* where Carey Mulligan goes back to her parents' house (after living the glamorous life with Peter Sarsgaard) and it seems so plain.

I love the part in *The Prince of Tides* where Nick Nolte admits he was abused and cries into Barbra Streisand's beige shoulder pad. I love that she cries one tear and her fingernails have French tips.

I love the part in *Coming Home* where Jane Fonda starts wearing her hair curly. Manuel loves the part where Jon Voight goes to her house for dinner and she has margaritas in the refrigerator ready to go. He thinks it's important to be a good hostess.

I love the part where Matthew McConaughey is shirtless in *Boys on the Side*. I remember him bouncing around in bed with Drew Barrymore and being envious that nothing on his body jiggled.

I love the part where Taye Diggs is shirtless in *How Stella Got Her Groove Back*.

I love the part where Colin Farrell is shirtless in *Tigerland*.

I love the part where Tobey Maguire is shirtless in *Spider-Man* (after the spider bite).

I love the part where Daniel Craig is shirtless in *Quantum of Solace*.

I love the part where Chris Evans is shirtless in *Fantastic Four*.

I love the part where Kevin Spacey is shirtless in *American Beauty*, and it looks like Wes Bentley is giving him head. (Really he's just leaning over to roll a joint.)

I love the part where Hugh Jackman is shirtless and pouring water on himself in *Australia*. Hugh Jackman crawled over me once in a movie theater on Houston Street. He sat two over from me, and I tried to act like it wasn't a big deal, but I was totally dying.

I love the part where we see Brad Pitt's butt in *Fight Club*.

I love the part where we see Ryan Phillippe's butt when he gets out of the pool in *Cruel Intentions*.

I love the part where we see William Baldwin's butt going up and down on Sharon Stone in *Sliver*.

I love the part where we see a hint of Gerard Butler's butt in *Law Abiding Citizen*.

I love the part where Colin Farrell weeps in *In Bruges*. I haven't seen the whole movie, but I keep coming across that scene on cable. He says something about shooting a little boy.

I love the part in *A Home at the End of the World* where Colin Farrell weeps while having sex with Robin Wright.

I love the part where Cher and Winona Ryder cry in *Mermaids*.

I love the part in *Courage Under Fire* where Denzel Washington cries a single tear.

I love the part in *Glory* where Denzel Washington cries a single tear.

I love the part in *Top Gun* where Tom Cruise and Kelly McGillis have shadowy sex in front of white curtains. I also love when they sloppy kiss on the back of his motorcycle.

I love the part in *The Wrestler* where Mickey Rourke sad-fucks the woman in the bathroom. I love the next morning that she has pictures of firemen plastered on her walls.

I love the part in *Margot at the Wedding* where the son tells Nicole Kidman he masturbated last night. It's as awkward as the time a poet rambled on about his unfaithful boyfriend at a publishing party. He was drunk and everyone quietly stood there eating cheese.

I love the part in *Easy Rider* when Dennis Hopper sits on the bed with the prostitute. When she crosses her leg, you can see the top of her fishnets and the bottom of her ass is cottage cheesy.

I love the part in *The Piano* where Sam Neill cuts off Holly Hunter's finger.

I love the part in *Boogie Nights* when Heather Graham smashes her roller skates into that guy's head.

I love the part in *Monster* where Charlize Theron shoots the nice guy (because it's so awful it's good).

I love the part in *Kill Bill: Vol. 2* where Uma Thurman kills David Carradine with her hand.

I love the part in *The Sixth Sense* where we find out Toni Collette's dead mom is proud of her.

I love the part in *Love! Valour! Compassion!* where we find out how they each will die.

I love the part in *Edward Scissorhands*: "If he weren't up there now, I don't think it would be snowing."

I love the part in *Rebel Without a Cause*: "He was always cold."

I love the part in *Milk*: "I just want you to know, Harvey, I'm really proud of you."

I love the part in *Stand by Me*: "I just wish that I could go some place where nobody knows me. I guess I'm just a pussy, huh?"

I love the part in *The Object of My Affection* where the guy with bushy eyebrows says to Paul Rudd: "I'll talk to you about poetry." It was the nineties, and I thought I could find that guy if I made a list of qualities I wanted in a man and thought positive thoughts. It wasn't true.

I love the part at the end of *The Graduate* where Dustin Hoffman and Katharine Ross are on the bus together. It's a good ending, but I do think it's weird that Katharine Ross wanted to be with someone who slept with her mother.

I love the part at the end of *Longtime Companion* where they reunite with their dead friends on the beach. I tried to find a T-shirt online like Stephen Caffrey was wearing, but I couldn't. Every time I go to Fire Island I think of that movie. (I also think of Frank O'Hara dying.)

4 • PRODIGAL

We pay for this later. I pay
for breakfast

—TIM DLUGOS

What It Feels Like to Be Aaron Smith

Though you would never admit it, you're still shocked by pubic hair in Diesel ads on Broadway and Houston, and you wonder what conversations lead up to a guy posing with his pants unzipped to the forest. Maybe the stylist does it, but somebody had to think, *let's show pubic hair,* and was that person nervous about saying, *hey, I have a great idea: pubic hair.* You think about David Leddick's book *Naked Men Too,* and the model with the cigarette whose mother photographed him with his jeans falling off and his pubic hair showing and how that's weird and you can't even begin to process how someone would let his own mother photograph him nearly naked and why a mother would want to. Everyone pretends pubic hair in pictures is artistic, but we all know it's really about sex, which you quickly remind yourself is okay, too, because you're liberal, which you sometimes think means you don't believe in anything because you want people to like you. Then you think how you hate the phrase *shock of pubic hair* in novels and spend the next several minutes trying to think of a better phrase, *shrub of . . . patch of . . . spread of . . . taste of . . . wad of . . .* then you think how Joyce Carol Oates describes fat men's chests as *melting chicken fat* in her story _____ and get paranoid because you used to be fat and can never get your chest as tight as you want no matter how much you bench press. You make a mental note to send poems to *Ontario Review,* Joyce Carol Oates is one of the editors and might like your work. They published Judith Vollmer's poem about the reporter covering a murder scene, and you love her and her poems (maybe you should send her an e-mail and see how she's doing). Then you think about pubic hair again, how embarrassing it can be at Dr. Engel's when he examines you and stares at it (do you have too much, how much can you trim and still look natural) both of you trying to pretend it's professional when he asks you to move into the light, holds your penis like a pencil, squeezes your balls, *this guy's fine, this guy's fine,* and you don't know how to be when he shakes your hand before you leave. Then you feel perverted because you're still thinking about pubic hair, maybe everyone has pubic hair issues and nobody talks about it? You know for a fact Laura does because she told you after she read a Sharon Olds poem out loud and the two of you giggled. You think of Tara, with thick eyeliner, who said well-groomed underarms are really sexy and you adopted that phrase when you say you think underarms are sexy, *well-groomed underarms* you say and friends agree, especially Tom who also loves underarms and sex clubs. You pass a hot guy (not as hot as the bag check guy at The Strand whose shirt comes up when he puts your backpack on the top shelf) and you want to sleep with him and stare, hoping he raises his arm so you can see his hair. You wonder if you have a disorder and then get mad as a taxi screams through your walk signal and think, *I understand why people open fire on playgrounds*, then you feel bad because it's not about children, even though they get on your nerves and nobody in Brooklyn disciplines their children, you pretend you didn't think that and think: *I understand why people open fire in public places* (like that's better). Then you get scared that maybe one day you'll snap and kill people, but probably not, then you're really scared that everyone feels like this and we don't realize how great the potential for disaster is, like yesterday walking between a car and bus on Fifth you trusted the bus driver to keep his foot on the brake and didn't worry he might pin you against the car and you'd end up like Christopher Reeve, immediately you try to decide if Christopher Reeve is a valid example of your fear or if you're just making fun of him, and you feel guilty, the way you feel guilty for laughing when Jeff says his messy apartment looks like Afghanistan, but you have to admit the metaphor of Superman becoming a quadriplegic is pretty amazing, but you probably shouldn't—no, you shouldn't write that.

Diesel Clothing Ad (Naked Man with Messenger Bag)

So what if the woman's hand reaching
for the bag pulls the bag

back and we see his dick,

that one ball hangs lower
than the other, that he shaves them.

So what. So what

if he likes her hand near
his dick and gets hard

and we see his red-tipped
dick taken in her fist

and her red-tipped
fingers gripping,
pulling: a hungry

dick in a hungry fist without
faces. So what if we do see

her face and his face and can tell
by his rolled-back eyes, her half-closed
eyes, that he wants her

to take him
in her mouth
and she wants to take him

and does, and we see that, too. So what.

So what if she's your daughter,
and he's somebody's son

and they like this sucking.
His hips jamming. Her head
nodding. Her throat

the hard red end of it.

And they like it. Both
of them. Both of them

like it. So what.

Antibiotic (West Virginia, 2010)

So I won't have to face a doctor,
won't have to get the speech, the look,
I pay out-of-pocket online.
I drive 45 minutes to the little clinic,
face one woman in a tiny room,
some plastic cups, a refrigerator:
No Food or Drinks, Specimens Only.

I know even this woman will judge,
but at least she won't make me
take my clothes off,
shove something up me,
make me wait on a table in socks.
I can pee in a cup in privacy.
I'm supposed to feel ashamed
like the first time I came
into a pillow while my parents
watched television in the basement.

When I sign in, she *does* judge,
says, *let me shut the door*
when she sees what I'm there for,
though the waiting room is empty.
She asks for ID, types
on her computer, is afraid
to put the ID back in my hand.
Is it my voice, my lack
of wedding ring, or the fact
I've had sex that makes her nervous?

I dated someone who is a liar, I say,
that's why I'm here.
Why do I forget who I am?
Why do I feel the need to get her to like me,
feel sorry for me, make up a story?
She nods, gets nicer. Relieved
I might be *normal.* Not a man

who had sex with a man he didn't know
on a living room floor.
I say to her: *I'm not a whore.*

Psalm (Boston)

I spilled out of the club
at dawn, the ones I'd come with

paired off and gone.
I walked up Berkeley toward

Beacon, toward the river,
home. The restaurant

on my left where I worked—
green awning, revolving door.

At that almost-hour details
don't matter, the Hancock

Tower an illusion of space,
mirrored and bragging

to the sky. I would
leave the city in a month.

Still jittery from cigarettes,
from pills that promised

escape, I fell inside my body—
the last place I wanted to be.

What I Wanted (Age 8)

I wanted Adam Nelson to coach
our intramural basketball team
with his shirt off. He was Kevin's
older brother, and I was full-
body tingle when he'd say my
name, tug my shorts, grunt *good play*.
I wanted eighth-grade boys
to wear mesh shirts and tank tops,
to throw big red balls into shiny,
wet arms. I wanted boys to hold
my hand like they did the girls.
I wanted them to tie me up and make
me kiss them. I wanted to cuddle
with Magnum P.I., put my chin on his
hairy chest and blow. I wanted Erik
Estrada on *CHiPs* to strip, to shoot
someone, then flash his armpits.
I wanted the men my dad hung out
with to walk around naked when we
camped. I wanted all men
in nothing but towels, to watch
them drop those towels in locker rooms
(oh locker rooms!). I wanted Tommy
Shaw to do push-ups and show me his
muscles. I wanted Ron Taylor to do
push-ups and show me his muscles.
I wanted Todd McCafferty to sit on my
lap and show me his muscles.
I wanted someone to show me
his muscles! I wanted to play
husband and wife, he'd be
the husband, and I'd be the wife.
I wanted boys to protect me
on the playground. I wanted boys
to chase me on the playground,
to shove their fingers in my
mouth, push me down.

Casino Royale, 2006 (The Blue Speedo and Daniel Craig)

One oiled-up stud;
one Lycra lick.

Blue cling
with an inside view,

the place something veiny
and strange is crammed into.

Christopher Street Pier (Evening)

When I think of New York,
I think of here: triangles of sailboats,
tourists posing against the railing:
Now find someone to take one together.
The sky over New Jersey is an explosion
of color, slashes of pink all through it.
I like when the city's behind me,
and I'm looking forward at all
that space: the Statue of Liberty
is a tiny green toy on my left,
the Lackawanna tower stands up
in front, to my right: another pier,
then more water, more water
and city. Planes circle in and out
of Newark, little lights getting bigger
as they approach. I make a wish
each time one passes over:
everything be okay for everyone.
Sometimes I just say: *Please.*
I moved here for the same reason
all gay men move here: to stop
struggling against what our bodies do
and with whom, but still I worry
all the time: will my sister get
what she wants, will Joel's cancer
come back, have I made a mistake
by living my life alone. Tonight
there are couples dancing under
a large white tent to music that sounds
like a record player, someone always
on the edge waiting for their turn.
If I died right now could I say
I've been happy? Though not very
long or completely or in any way
I can explain, I could say, yeah,
I think I've been happy.

Prodigal

This morning I yelled at a student for texting in class.
Put that away, I don't want to see it.
I wanted to scream: *Get fucked.*
I wanted to humiliate her, make her feel how I feel:
There's the faggot professor. They don't say it like that,
but I feel the looks, the not-quite-whispered whispers,
the disgust of what I do with men
cracked across their faces. I want to say:
It's all true. There's nowhere I won't put a cock,
and I see a lot of me in you.
Am I really back in West Virginia?
Did I really leave New York City?
It's hard to remember,
here where everything is green.
I was afraid I'd get AIDS from the toilet seat,
I heard a girl say on the street my first day in town.
And in the store with the confederate flags
I interrupted a joke: *How many fags,* big laugh,
Oh, can I help you?
A person who lives in the same state
as his parents, one of three gay men in a tiny college town,
someone who thinks he's always dying:
so many things I never wanted to be again.
It doesn't work like that, I tell the students.
It's not A to B to C. It's over and over and all at once.
But it's hard to see that
past all these trees, fucking trees.

5 · APPETITE

I love this hairy city.

—FRANK O'HARA

Appetite

That was the summer
I carried a kitchen knife

for protection and slammed
my car into the truck

of a man who stood me up
at a bar. What else could

I do after so much
religion? I got stoned

in the bathroom before
work, and my roommate

spent our rent money on
cigarettes and CDs. Dance

music and AIDS tests
and married men: one

with a crucifix that dangled
in my face when he

straddled me, who said *show
me your dick* while his

kids slept on a foldout
couch in the basement.

I fantasized every heat-heavy
glance into a love story and

stole ice-cream sandwiches
from a convenience store

on Murray Avenue. It was
Pittsburgh. I was hungry.

Make Him Think You Could Pull a Gun

Make him think you're crazy, make him think
        you could pull a gun. He'll remember you
                this way. Men respond to grand gestures,

men respond, in their deepest parts, to fear.
        Tell him you've met before, you're sure of it,
                you never forget a face

twisted in pleasure, panic. Watch his mouth dissolve,
        watch it betray him. Show him a knife
                slicing a body (more surprise than pain).

He'll pretend he's comfortable,
        that you really don't scare him. But it's all an anxious
                lie. You've seen the movies,

and every scene is your scene:
        the psycho singing love songs to the man he loves,
                blood, a perfect sunset, on the dead mother's cheek—

you can taste that light. Tell him nobody belongs to him
        more than you. Let him think he has some
                room. Let him think he can choose.

Notes on Contributors

Jose Y. (First Time)

He wouldn't take his pants off
because he didn't like his legs.
A place below his right nipple tasted sour.
I saw foggy rainbows in the lights after he left
from leaving my contacts in too long.

• • •

Mark C. (with Cher)

He invited me over for dinner (fancy pizza).
I made him come first—he shuddered like he was freezing.
We watched *Will & Grace* (first Cher episode).
He ruined my dry-clean-only Gap sweater.

• • •

Mark F. (Closeted)

He asked me to take my clothes off while he sat on the couch.
He asked me to turn in a circle so he could look at me.
He asked me to leave.

• • •

George P. (with Soundtrack)

He played the Selena album.
I came in his mouth.

• • •

Philippe C. (First Loss)

I coughed all night with a summer cold.
He licked my pre-cum off his hand.
I lay there the next morning and watched him sleep.
He said *god dangles people in our faces, then tells us we can't have them.*
He used his underwear to clean our bodies.

• • •

Rob ? (Bored)

He said all you have to do is kiss me and stick it in me.
I told him I wouldn't do either.

• • •

Brian S. (Dark, Older Man)

He was cocky like Bruce Willis.
He took my cock in his mouth like he was starving.
We talked about Szymborska and *New York Review of Books*.
He lay naked on the bed to watch me dress.
We shook hands when we met.

What Christians Say During Sex

The hipster christians are rolling their jeans up
        making shorts out of pants, making fashion
out of fashion, and I'm watching it all happen
        in a coffee shop called Ugly Mugs,
and I haven't seen a mug since I got here
        (paper cups and cookies served
on recycled napkins). A disappointingly straight
        man is talking to another straight man
about Christ, about *devotion to the Lord*
        while his wife sits beside them on the couch
staring out the wall-length windows
        at the street, the trees, the sun drooping in
and out of clouds. She smiles because
        she's proud of him. She smiles because
there's nothing to say. He has beautiful arms,
        the kind that would glisten if he did push-ups
with his shirt off, or someone nailed him
        to a cross. *I shaved my head last night*,
he says, and I look at his ears to see if the line
        is even. I wonder if they talk dirty
during sex? Does she say, *I need you to fuck me?*
        Does he say, *I want to eat your pussy?*
Or is it a sin to say it like that even when you're
        married? *I'm looking for someone,*
he says, *to play guitar for my band, someone
        committed to Christ.* I wonder what they
smell like after sex? I wonder what Jesus
        does for them, what they think Christ's
face will look like when they get to heaven?

The Earth Spins Toward Oblivion While We Ride Trains

We all crowd in to stare at each other
and to read our free newspapers
and to nod in our headphones

the way those who can't get enough of Jesus
nod when they're told more about Jesus.

Our socks fall down in our boots,
our underwear twists up our butts and needs fixing.

A man in jeans says something
to a man in dress pants about *the game.*

Dress Pants (who is white) says the Jets kicked ass
and because he wants Jeans (who is black) to understand
he hands him his newspaper
and they are both resplendent with connection.

They could have just been kissed!
They have that kind of look on their faces!

Jeans starts to read about the game-that-kicked-ass
and Dress Pants spreads his legs to scratch.

Against the door Receding Hairline hides his erection
and Too Much Jewelry smells her finger.
Talking across me High-Heeled Boots
tells Last Year's Hair about that

sorry sonofabitch she's living with—
she swears she can't go on like this,
not for one more fucking second.

Anonymous

I don't have an American
body, I have an anonymous body . . .

—FRANK O'HARA

Inside the room he's pulled
the-other-he's pants down.

Before they suck, before they
fuck each other in the apartment

with no curtains (windows
facing a dirty brick wall), they

spit their anonymous tongues
into the other's anonymous

mouth because they don't want
to speak, no *where are you from*

no *love me in the morning*.
The couples outside are married

to their bad decisions: gold bands
and strollers, men and women.

They're two *hims* in a bedroom
off Second Avenue and it's summer.

They are grab and grab, suck
and thrust, is that his cock?

Is that *his* cock? They are chest
to chest, stomach to stomach,

his hand on his ass, then him
on his knees, then him on his

back his cock in his ass, and him
on his back and his cock, back

and forth, him, then him, then
him, him, him, then him again.

Psalm (West Virginia)

These days when it's raining
and I wish it were over: the winter, the year,
the students' random commas
like shaved-away hair, I think: now is the time
before it all goes bad: a lump
not found, a spot on the skin, a dizziness
deep inside the brain. Cars pass
like little trains, but less ambitious, and I wonder
if I'll wish for this: pillow of gray sky
smothering me, the mist on my glasses
making it hard to see. No real tragedies to make me
unhappy. I'm told I'm depressed, but I think I'm crazy
with loneliness, from too many bad
decisions. Today I say: hurry up, go faster, I don't care
what happens. I'm willing to regret it all.

West Side Highway (Meditation)

This evening New York looks
how it always looks in photos

except more flawed, like someone picked it up
and didn't put it back the way they found it.

This far west the buildings could slip
into the Hudson, and who would miss them,

miss me? This far west it's all construction,
someone's good idea, each high-rise

becomes another high-rise stacked
against the soon-to-be-black sky.

Twilight's only bearable in the city,
lights making something different

than daylight, little lies saying,
you're not really alone.

This is the life we asked for,
and it's everything we expected.

There's nowhere else so light
and dark at the same time.

Because there's nowhere to go
when we die, our lives really can

be summed up by so many buildings
between two rivers, and because

they're unfinished, the sky behind
glows pink and gray inside them.

Train (Hymn)

The man across from me on the blue plastic seat
is the color of Brandon's new boots

and lovely
reading Che Guevara

I want him also to be
a revolutionary

to rail against government
end poverty

to eat peanut butter sandwiches
in bed

(look at me)

NOTES

"Men in Groups" is in conversation with David Groff's poem "The White Boy Pulls Down His Pants."

"Lucky" is for Stacey Waite.

"Film Short: Husband and Wife in a Grocery Store" is in memory of Irene McKinney.

"The Problem with Straight People (What We Say Behind Your Back)" is for Celeste Gainey and James Allen Hall.

"After All These Years You Know They Were Wrong about the Sadness of Men Who Love Men" is for Matt Nitowski.

"I Love the Part" is for Manuel Muñoz.

"*Casino Royale*, 2006 (The Blue Speedo and Daniel Craig)" is for Randall Mann.

"Christopher Street Pier (Evening)" owes a debt to Ed Ochester's "On Frank O'Hara's Birthday, Key West." It is dedicated to Chip Livingston.

"Appetite" is for RJ Gibson, who gave me the title.

"West Side Highway (Meditation)" is for Steven Alvarado.

The trivia in "*Fatal Attraction*, 1987 (Movie Review and Trivia)" and "*Boogie Nights*, 1997 (Movie Review and Trivia)" comes from the International Movie Database (imdb.com) and other various websites. I have no idea if all the information is true.

ACKNOWLEDGMENTS

Grateful acknowledgment is made to the editors of the following publications in which some of these poems previously appeared (sometimes in different versions):

Columbia Poetry Review ("Hurtful," "Prodigal," "The Problem with Straight People [What We Say Behind Your Back]"); *Court Green* ("Diesel Clothing Ad [Naked Man with Messenger Bag]," "The Earth Spins Toward Oblivion While We Ride Trains," "Fire Island, June 2008," "I Love the Part," "Notes on Contributors," "West Side Highway [Meditation]," "What Christians Say During Sex," "What I Wanted [Age 8]," "What It Feels Like to Be Aaron Smith"); *Ecotone* ("After All These Years You Know They Were Wrong about the Sadness of Men Who Love Men"); *5 AM* ("Men in Groups"); *Gulf Coast* ("Appetite"); *LI* ("Jesus Poem [Pierre et Gilles]"); *MiPoesias* ("Casino Royale, 2006 [The Blue Speedo and Daniel Craig]"); *Nepotist* ("Make Him Think You Could Pull a Gun"); *Ploughshares* ("Fat Ass"); *Witness* ("Lucky," "Psalm [Queer]").

The following poems appeared in the chapbook *Men in Groups* published by Winged City Press (an imprint of New Sins Press): "Men in Groups," "Lucky," "Psalm (Queer)," "Hurtful," "Film Short: Husband and Wife in a Grocery Store," "He Only Reads Fiction," "Celebrity Photo (Daniel Craig w/ Angelina Jolie)," "After All These Years You Know They Were Wrong about the Sadness of Men Who Love Men," "Diesel Clothing Ad (Naked Man with Messenger Bag)," "*Casino Royale*, 2006 (The Blue Speedo and Daniel Craig)," "Appetite," "Make Him Think You Could Pull a Gun," "The Earth Spins Toward Oblivion While We Ride Trains," and "West Side Highway (Meditation)."

"Train (Hymn)" and "The Earth Spins Toward Oblivion While We Ride Trains" appeared in *Token Entry: New York City Subway Poems* (Smalls Press), edited by Gerry LaFemina.

I would like to thank my friends and family. I particularly want to thank my sister, Belinda, for her steadfast support and Nancy Krygowski for our friendship and history. Thank you, Ed Ochester and the University of Pittsburgh Press. I am especially grateful to Jan Beatty. This book wouldn't exist without her thoughtfulness, dedication, and nudging.